DRIVEWAY HOOPS

AN ILLUSTRATED GUIDE TO BASKETBALL FUNDAMENTALS FOR KIDS, PARENTS, AND COACHES

DRIVEWAY HOOPS
An Illustrated Guide to Basketball Fundamentals
for Kids, Parents, and Coaches

ISBN 979-8-9852509-0-9 (hardcover)
eISBN 979-8-9852509-1-6 (ebook)
First edition 2022
Printed in the United States of America

Advize Proactive Consulting, LLC
83 Seacord Road
New Rochelle NY 10804
coachjonathanhalpert.com

Interior illustrations by Sari Kopitnikoff
Cover and book interior design by Andrea Leigh Ptak
Copyediting/Proofreading by Nancy Silk

TABLE OF CONTENTS

DEDICATED TO

Bernard "Red" Sarachek

Former St. John's basketball coach Lou Carnesecca once observed, "Red Sarachek has taught more high school and college coaches in the New York metro area than anybody. He was the guru." At Yeshiva University where Red coached from 1945 to 1969, he was simply labeled the "Rebbe," the "master." Coaches from throughout the New York metro area came to absorb Red's insights on "moving without the ball," and every Yeshiva College practice was a coaching clinic. If you arrived early, you could enjoy the extra bonus of watching Red work with Power Memorial Academy coach Jack Donohue and his star freshman Lew Alcindor (Kareem Abdul-Jabbar).

L to R: Johnny Halpert and Red Sarachek, February 1966

When professional basketball was in its infancy in the 1940s, Sarachek simultaneously coached the Scranton Miners of the American Basketball League and Herkimer in the New York State League and led both teams to championships while coaching at Yeshiva University.

With Scranton in the late '40s, Sarachek broke the league's segregation rules by playing Dolly King, William "Pop" Gates, and Eddie Younger at the same time. Pop Gates went on to a pro career that led to international fame with the Harlem Globetrotters and enshrinement in the NBA Hall of Fame.

In 1992, Red moved to Florida and we started a twenty-year AT&T ritual. In the off-season we would speak twice a week and in-season we would talk before and after every game. The ritual was always the same. If I called him after 10 a.m. the next morning, he would answer the phone yelling, "How could you lose to those guys?"

"How did you know we lost?" I would ask.

"When you win, you call before ten."

During those phone conversations, Red would implore me to "Write it all down. I want people to know." This book is dedicated to Red and represents the fulfillment of my promise that I would write it all down so that Red's knowledge and insights would be preserved for future coaches.

Beyond his knowledge of the game, Red was a man of great strength and courage. The strength that accrues from truth and the courage to act on the truth. Red possessed both of those qualities.

I think of Red every day. I miss him very much.

IN TRIBUTE TO

Lou Carnesecca

Lou Carnesecca's success at St. John's University and the New York Nets coupled with his enshrinement in the Basketball Hall of Fame all testify to his status as a legendary coach. However, beyond his great achievements on the court, Coach Carnesecca is a man of great loyalty and friendship and never allowed a personal moment of triumph to pass without acknowledging "Red's" contribution to his career triumphs. Beyond being a great coach, Lou is a man who has always followed the dictum "Let the honor of your friend be as dear to you as your own…" (*Sayings of the Fathers*, Chapter 2, sentence 15).

PREFACE
The Fundamentals of Playing with the Ball

All ideas and endeavors continually evolve. The game of basketball is no exception. In the 1940s, players weaved and took set shots, in the 1960s they picked and took jump shots, and today they hoist step-back threes off crossover dribbles. Although these new skills continue to transform the game, they remain the product of the fundamentals of how to dribble, pass, and shoot.

Player development ultimately requires athleticism as defined by agility and quickness, but it is the fundamentals that enable the less gifted player to neutralize his more skilled opponent. More importantly, it is the fundamentals that give kids, regardless of their skill level, the opportunity to compete and experience moments of triumph in front of family and friends.

Every child needs something that fuels feelings of self-worth. That "something" can be academic awards, playing the piano, growing tomatoes, or even making a game-winning foul shot. How children feel about themselves is fundamental to their psychological well-being. Therefore, children must not only have the opportunity to hear cheers in their classrooms but also to receive high fives from friends in the schoolyard. The amount of time parents spend in their driveways teaching their children how to shoot foul shots and layups is evidence that parents recognize that sports can be that "something."

Through the use of illustration, *Driveway Hoops* attempts to help parents and children learn the fundamentals of basketball, not to garner athletic scholarships, but to give all kids the opportunity to hear their friends and parents yell, "Good shot!"

CHAPTER 1
Body Balance

For a player to pivot, pass, or shoot, his body must be balanced and not leaning in one direction, similar to when he is learning to ride a bike. A player maintains body balance by keeping his knees partially bent, which automatically lifts his heels slightly off the floor and transfers his weight to his toes.

Knees slightly bent

Heels slightly off the floor

Weight on toes

If you want to test the accuracy of this concept, hold a ball at your waist. Your weight immediately shifts to the front of your feet, and your body is balanced and ready to attack your opponent. If you raise the ball up behind your head, causing your body to lean back slightly and away from the basket, your weight will shift to your heels and off your toes, making it difficult to walk, let alone attack your defender.

CHAPTER 2
Square to the Basket
At the Top of the Key

Whether a player is pivoting, passing, or shooting, her body must not only be balanced but must also be facing the basket. Or, to use the vernacular, the player must be **square to the basket**. To be square, both feet must be parallel, and the midpoint of the player's body and feet must intersect the midpoint of the rim. A player's body and feet must be square to the basket because feet, like car wheels, can only take you in the direction they are facing.

On the Left Wing

Left wing

On the Right Wing

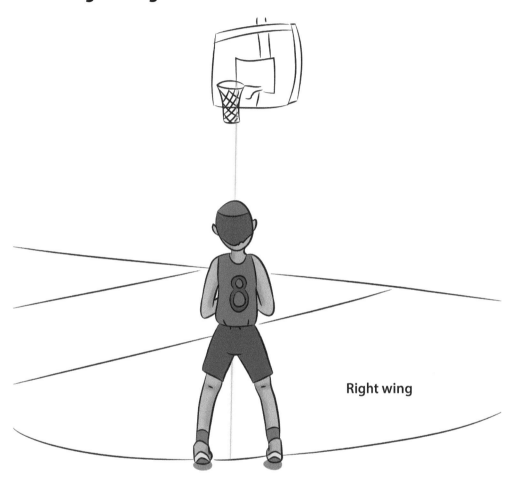

Right wing

CHAPTER 3
Creating a Pivot Foot
Left Foot

When a player lifts one foot off the floor, the other foot automatically becomes the pivot foot and cannot be lifted off the floor unless accompanied by a dribble. Although the pivot foot cannot be lifted off the floor, it can be **swiveled** by spinning on the toes of the pivot foot. Once again, it is important to maintain body weight on the toes, because you cannot swivel when you are standing flat-footed.

Pivot foot

Left Foot Pivot

A player can pivot right or swivel his foot to the right.

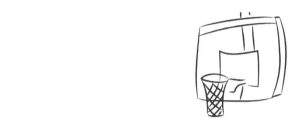

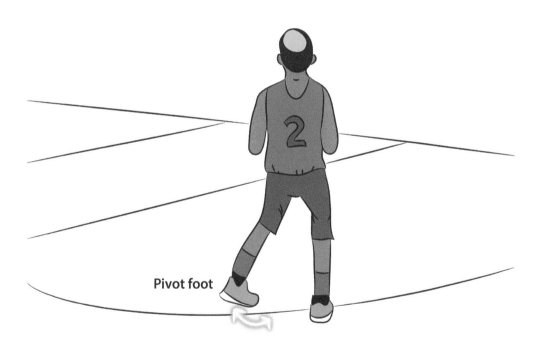

Pivot foot

Left Foot Pivot

A player can pivot left or swivel his foot to the left.

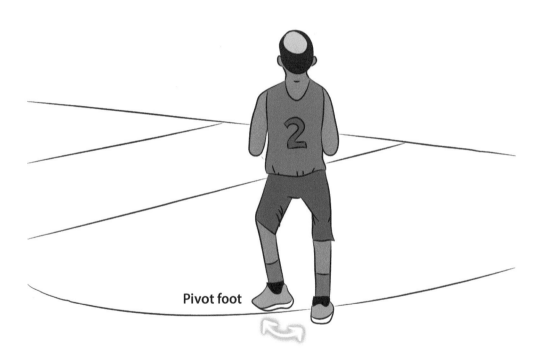

Pivot foot

Left Foot Pivot

The player simultaneously swings his body and right foot to the left.

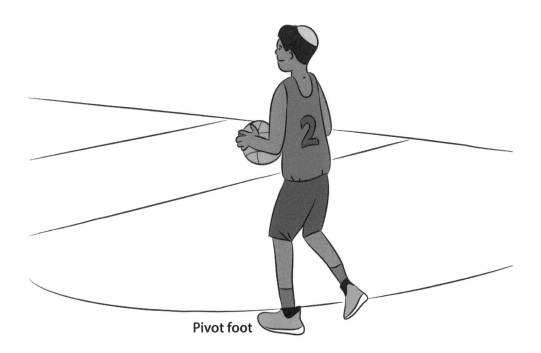

Pivot foot

Left Foot Pivot

The player has completed his pivot and is now square and prepared to pass the ball to a teammate.

Left Foot Pivot

Full sequence of pivoting to the left…and pivoting back to be square to the basket

Creating a Pivot Foot
Right Foot

When a player lifts one foot off the floor, the other foot automatically becomes the pivot foot and cannot be lifted off the floor unless accompanied by a dribble. Although the pivot foot cannot be lifted off the floor, it can be **swiveled** by spinning on the toes of the pivot foot. Once again, it is important to maintain body weight on the toes, because you cannot swivel when you are standing flat-footed.

Pivot foot

Right Foot Pivot

A player can pivot left or swivel her foot to the left.

Pivot foot

Right Foot Pivot

A player can pivot right or swivel her foot to the right.

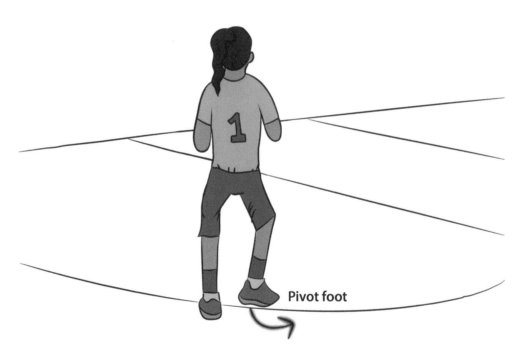

Pivot foot

Right Foot Pivot

The player simultaneously swings her body and left foot to the right.

Pivot foot

Right Foot Pivot

The player has completed her pivot and is now square and prepared to pass the ball to a teammate.

Right Foot Pivot

Full sequence of pivoting to the right...and pivoting back to be square to the basket

CHAPTER 4
Jab Step to Create Space

Once the player has established the pivot foot, he can now employ the other foot to **jab step in the neutral zone**, the area between the offensive and defensive player. The **jab step** is a short, hard step that shifts the defender's balance away from the offensive player and creates space for the offensive player to pass, dribble, and shoot.

Jab Step LEFT Foot

The player jab steps **left** with his left foot, his non-pivot foot.

Jab foot

The neutral zone

Jab Step LEFT Foot

The player jab steps **forward** with his left foot, his non-pivot foot.

Jab foot

Jab Step LEFT Foot

The player jab steps **across his body** with his left foot, his non-pivot foot.

Jab foot

Jab Step RIGHT Foot

The player jab steps **right** with her right foot, her non-pivot foot.

Jab foot

The neutral zone

Jab Step RIGHT Foot

The player jab steps **forward** with her right foot, her non-pivot foot.

Jab foot

Jab Step RIGHT Foot

The player jab steps **across her body** with her right foot, her non-pivot foot.

Jab foot

CHAPTER 5

Swing the Ball to Create Space

The offensive player can also create space between himself and his defender by swinging the ball right to left through the neutral zone.

CHAPTER 6
Practice Drill
Be Square-Freeze-Jab-Create Space

Scan this QR code for a video of the Practice Drills that incorporate the fundamentals of "Body Balance, Being Square, Pivoting, and Creating Space" illustrated in Chapters 1 through 5.

The player identifies five locations on the court, two to the right of the key, two to the left of the key, and one at the top of the key.

● The player starts in the right corner and moves clockwise from location to location.

Throw – Hop – Face Up – Freeze – Jab – Create Space

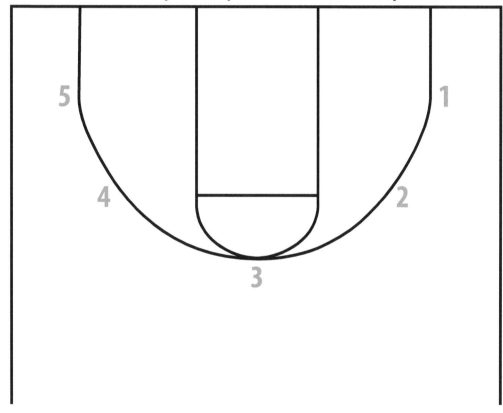

Instructions

- When the player is moving from location 1 to location 5, the player establishes the **RIGHT FOOT** as the **PIVOT FOOT**.

- When the player is moving from location 5 back to 1, the player establishes the **LEFT FOOT** as the **PIVOT FOOT**.

- The player starts at the first location, the right corner.

- The player throws a self-pass.

- The player hops to the ball and faces up.

- The player freezes the defender.

- The player jab steps **left** to create space.

- The player jab steps **forward** to create space.

- The player jab steps **back** to create space.

- The player continues to move in rapid succession from location 1 to location 5 and then back from location 5 to location 1.

- The player should repeat this full drill two to three times.

THROW a Self-Pass:

- The player throws a self-pass by holding the ball at his waist, with each hand on one side of the ball and the seams of the ball running horizontally.

- The player flips the ball in the air slightly above his head with a reverse spin, aiming the ball so it will bounce at the next marked location.

- The reverse spin will cause the ball to bounce back toward the player. The player does not throw the ball as if he is making a pass and throwing the ball away, but flips the ball into the air with a reverse spin so that when the ball bounces, it will bounce back toward the player who threw the pass.

FACE UP – Hop to the Ball:

- As the ball hits the next location on the floor, the player hops toward the bouncing ball, simulating that he is receiving a pass.

- The hop is not a jump, as if the player is trying to jump for a rebound, but is a small hop with the player's feet approximately two to three inches off the floor.

- The player hops and catches the ball, simultaneously landing on both feet and facing the basket. If the player lands on both feet simultaneously, he will not have a pivot foot. If the player lands on only one foot, that foot will automatically become his pivot foot.

FREEZE the Defender:

- Upon landing at the next location, the player must be square to the basket, which means that his feet and body must be facing the basket and not turned sideways.

- The player's feet must be parallel, not too close together and not too far apart.

- The player should be holding the ball slightly below the waist.

- In this position, the player comes to a complete stop for a full second and **freezes the defender.**

JAB Step – CREATE SPACE

- The player jab steps with the non-pivot foot to create space in the neutral zone, the area between the offensive player and the defender.

CHAPTER 7

Scan this QR code for a video of the fundamentals of "Pivoting and Passing."

Pivoting and Passing
To the Left

When making a pass, the player should dribble toward the recipient of the pass. This dribble can influence the recipient's defender to turn his head toward the ball and cause him to lose sight of the recipient of the pass.

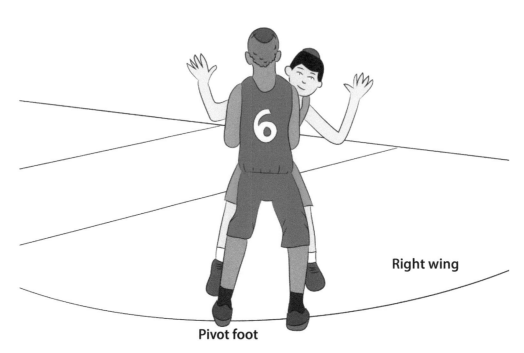

Right wing

Pivot foot

Player #6 is square to the basket and has proper body balance.

Pivoting and Passing to the Left

Player #6 pivots on his left foot to protect the ball with his body as he begins to swing his right foot, his jab foot, across his body.

Pivot foot   **Jab foot**

Pivoting and Passing to the Left

Player #6 has completed his pivot and is now square to the recipient of the pass.

Jab foot

Pivoting and Passing to the Left

Player #6 steps with his right foot, protecting the ball with his body, and follows through by making a full extension of his arms and hands.

Jab foot

Pivot foot

Pivoting and Passing to the Left

Full sequence of pivoting and passing to the left

1. Square to basket

2. Pivot left foot

3. Swing right foot

4. Follow-through

Pivoting and Passing
To the Right

When making a pass, the player should dribble toward the recipient of the pass. This dribble can influence the recipient's defender to turn her head toward the ball and cause her to lose sight of the recipient of the pass.

Left wing

Player #31 is square to the basket and has proper body balance.

Pivoting and Passing to the Right

Player #31 pivots on her right foot to protect the ball with her body as she begins to swing her left foot, her jab foot, across her body.

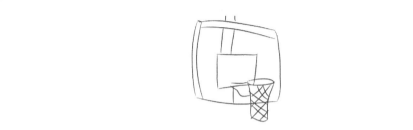

Jab foot

Pivot foot

Pivoting and Passing to the Right

Player #31 has completed her pivot and is now square to the recipient of the pass.

Jab foot

Pivoting and Passing to the Right

#31 steps with her left foot, protecting the ball with her body, and follows through by making a full extension of her arms and hands.

Jab foot

Pivot foot

Pivoting and Passing to the Right

Full sequence of pivoting and passing to the right

1. Square to basket

2. Pivot right foot

3. Swing left foot

4. Follow-through

CHAPTER 8

Scan this QR code for a video of the fundamentals of "Passing Against the Defender's Hands."

Passing Against the Defender's Hands

The Bounce Pass

The passer holds the ball with one hand on either side of the ball and protects the ball with his body by jab stepping with his jab foot. The passer follows through on his pass by making a full extension of his arms and hands. If the defender's hands are up, the passer makes a bounce pass.

The Chest Pass

If the defender's hands are down, the passer makes a chest pass.

Bounce Pass

Jab foot

Pivot foot

Chest Pass

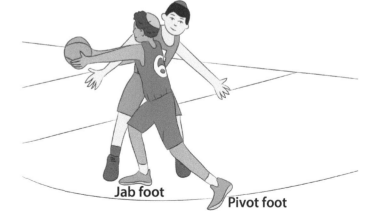

Jab foot

Pivot foot

The Baseline Pass

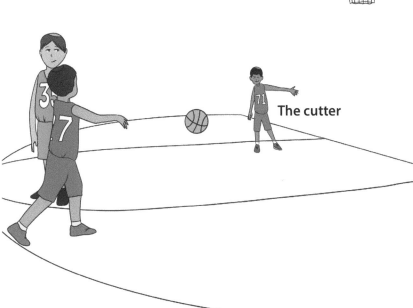

The cutter

The passer must throw the ball **in front of the player** cutting to the basket so the cutter can catch the ball without breaking his momentum toward the basket. On the right side of the court, the passer throws to the cutter while pivoting on his right foot and swinging his left foot toward the basket.

If the passer pivots on his left foot and swings his right foot, he will throw the ball **behind the cutter,** forcing the player to reach back for the ball and interrupt his cut to the basket.

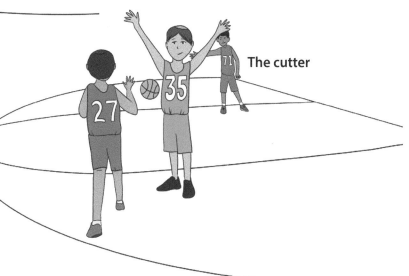

The cutter

CHAPTER 9
Flash and Face Up

Bringing (flashing) a player to the "up-bucket" position, the area near the foul line, enables the team to utilize both sides of the court while also limiting double team (two players on the ball) opportunities.

To successfully gain the up-bucket position, the player must first:

- Play chest to chest against his defensive player

- Jab step in the opposite direction that he is cutting

- Cut on a diagonal line

Upon flashing (cutting), to the up-bucket position, the cutter will have his back to the basket and must therefore face up before he can become an offensive threat.

The player faces up by swiveling on his pivot foot, his left foot.

Pivot foot

Jab foot   Pivot foot

The player is now facing the basket and in position to initiate the offense from either side of the court.

CHAPTER 10

Receiving the Pass

Scan this QR code for a video of the fundamentals of "Receiving the Pass."

Player #4, who is receiving the pass, cannot stand still waiting for the pass, but must move toward the ball or, to use the vernacular, must jump or **hop to meet the pass.**

Player #4, the player receiving the pass, must first jab step away from the passer...

Jab step away

and then after jab stepping must simultaneously pivot and hop (jump) to meet the pass.

As player #4 is in the air waiting to receive the pass, he simultaneously turns his body so that upon catching the ball and landing on the floor he will be square to the basket.

Jab foot

Pivot foot

Player #4 is now square to the basket and has the opportunity to choose a pivot foot and attack his defender via a pass drive or shot. If Player #4 lands with one foot on the floor, that foot automatically becomes his pivot foot.

Freeze the Defender

A frequent mistake players make is to dribble the ball immediately upon receiving the pass. Basketball is not football, where the player scores by running across a fifty-yard-wide goal line. In basketball, the goal is to get to a nineteen-inch cylinder centered on a fifty-foot end line, ten feet off the ground. Therefore, the first thing a player must do upon receiving a pass is **NOTHING** except **freeze the defender.** Dribbling as soon as you receive the ball denies you the opportunity to see how your defender is guarding you and often will result in your dribbling away from the basket. By first **freezing the defender**, the offensive player can insure that he will be in balance, square to the basket, under control, and able to employ all of his offensive options.

Full sequence of jumping to meet the pass and freezing the defender

Square to the basket

Jab step

Jump to meet the pass

Catching and turning the body

Face up ready to attack

CHAPTER 11
Drive to the Basket
Right Side

Scan this QR code for a video of the fundamentals of "Drive to the Basket, the Rule of Five Steps."

Some players are blessed with the athleticism of a quick first step. However, players who lack initial explosiveness can still beat their defender to the basket by:

- Being square to the basket
- Maintaining proper body balance
- **Executing the rule of FIVE STEPS**

Player #19 is square to the basket and maintaining proper body balance.

Jab foot

Pivot foot

Drive to the Basket – Right Side

STEP 1: THE JAB STEP

Player #19 jab steps with his left foot to shift the defender's balance to the right.

Jab foot

Pivot foot

Drive to the Basket – Right Side

STEP 2 : THE STEP ACROSS THE BODY

Player #19 simultaneously initiates his dribble and steps across his body with his left foot, his jab foot. The dribble must be made **in front** of his jab foot, not to his side, and must not be higher than his waist.

Pivot foot   **Jab foot**

Drive to the Basket – Right Side
THE DRIBBLE AND STEP 2 ARE NOW COMPLETE.

Step 1 and Step 2 are the greatest challenge young children face in learning how to drive to the basket because the player must simultaneously coordinate the step across his body with his initial dribble. A failure to step properly or dribbling too late will inevitably result in the player's momentum taking him away from the basket or shooting off the wrong foot.

Step 1 – The Jab Step   **Step 2 – The Step Across the Body**   **The Dribble**

Drive to the Basket – Right Side

STEP 3: THE PIVOT FOOT

Following the dribble, player #19 steps **toward the basket** with his pivot foot, his right foot, as he cradles the ball in his right hand.

Success in completing the drive is based on the player stepping **toward the basket**. If the player steps to the right, the drive will take the player to the side of the backboard and not to the rim.

Pivot foot

**Incorrect step to the right
and not toward the rim**

Drive to the Basket – Right Side

STEP 4: THE JAB FOOT

Player #19 steps with his **left foot**, his **jab foot**, and begins to lift his body off the floor by pushing off of his **right foot**, his **pivot foot**.

Jab foot

Drive to the Basket – Right Side

Right Foot, Right Hand

Player #19 lifts his **right foot**, his **pivot foot**, and prepares to shoot the ball with his **right hand**.

Pivot foot

Drive to the Basket – Right Side

RELEASE AND FOLLOW-THROUGH

Right Foot, Right Hand

Player #19 rises off the floor and shoots the ball with his **right hand** with a complete follow-through.

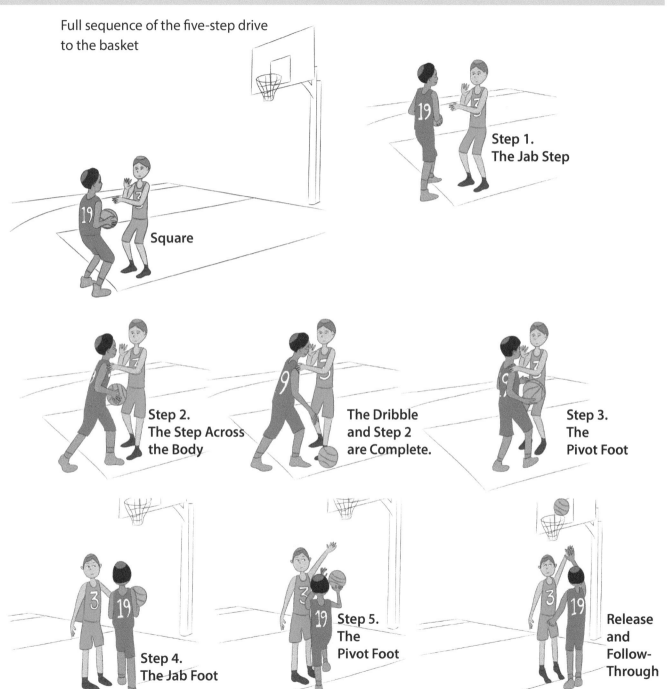

Full sequence of the five-step drive to the basket

Step 1.
The Jab Step

Square

Step 2.
The Step Across
the Body

The Dribble
and Step 2
are Complete.

Step 3.
The
Pivot Foot

Step 4.
The Jab Foot

Step 5.
The
Pivot Foot

Release
and
Follow-
Through

Practice Drill
Five Steps to the Basket

Scan this QR code for a video of the fundamentals of "Drive to the Basket, the Rule of Five Steps."

The five-step drive to the basket should be taught in the following stages:

- The player should first practice the **step across the body** without a ball by **simultaneously stepping and simulating a dribble**.

- Once the player has learned to coordinate the step with the dribble, he can introduce the ball and practice the step with one dribble. The player must remember to dribble the ball below the waist and in front of the jab step.

- After the player demonstrates that he can simultaneously coordinate the **crossover step** with the **dribble**, the player simulates steps 3, 4, and 5 by walking and counting each step out loud. The player finishes the walking drive by simulating a shot.

- Once the player has demonstrated that he has coordinated all five steps to the basket with only one dribble and is shooting off the correct foot, he can practice the entire five-step drive at game speed.

Drive to the Basket – Left Side

Some players are blessed with the athleticism of a quick first step. However, players who lack initial explosiveness can still beat their defender to the basket by:

- Being square to the basket
- Maintaining proper body balance
- **Executing the rule of FIVE STEPS**

Player #12 is square to the basket and maintaining proper body balance.

Drive to the Basket – Left Side

STEP 1: THE JAB STEP

Player #12 jab steps with her right foot to shift the defender's balance to the left.

Jab foot

Drive to the Basket – Left Side

STEP 2: THE STEP ACROSS THE BODY

Player #12 simultaneously initiates her dribble and steps across her body with her right foot, her jab foot. The dribble must be made **in front** of her jab foot, not to her side, and must not be higher than her waist.

Jab foot   Pivot foot

Drive to the Basket – Left Side
THE DRIBBLE AND STEP 2 ARE NOW COMPLETE.

Step 1 and Step 2 are the greatest challenge young children face in learning how to drive to the basket because the player must simultaneously coordinate the step across her body with her initial dribble. A failure to step properly or dribbling too late will inevitably result in the player's momentum taking her away from the basket or shooting off the wrong foot.

Jab foot

Step 1 – The Jab Step   **Step 2 – The Step Across the Body**   **The Dribble**

Drive to the Basket – Left Side

STEP 3: THE PIVOT FOOT

Following the dribble, player #12 steps **toward the basket** with her pivot foot, her left foot, as she cradles the ball in her left hand.

Success in completing the drive is based on the player stepping **toward the basket**. If the player steps to the left, the drive will take the player to the side of the backboard and not to the rim.

Pivot foot

Incorrect step to the left
and not toward the rim

Drive to the Basket – Left Side

STEP 4: THE JAB FOOT

Player #12 steps with her **right foot**, her **jab foot**, and begins to lift her body off the floor by pushing off of her **left foot**, her **pivot foot**.

Jab foot

Drive to the Basket – Left Side

Left Foot, Left Hand

Player #12 lifts her **left foot**, her **pivot foot**, and prepares to shoot the ball with her **left hand.**

Pivot foot

Drive to the Basket – Left Side

RELEASE AND FOLLOW-THROUGH

Left Foot, Left Hand

Player #12 rises off the floor and shoots the ball with her **left hand** with a complete follow-through.

Full sequence of the five-step drive to the basket

Square

Step 1.
The Jab Step

Step 2.
The Step Across
the Body

The Dribble
and Step 2
are Complete.

Step 3.
The Pivot Foot

Step 4.
The Jab Foot

Step 5.
The Pivot Foot

Release and
Follow-Through

Practice Drill
Five Steps to the Basket

Scan this QR code for a video of the fundamentals of "Drive to the Basket, the Rule of Five Steps."

The five-step drive to the basket should be taught in the following stages:

- The player should first practice the **step across the body** without a ball by **simultaneously stepping and simulating a dribble**.

- Once the player has learned to coordinate the step with the dribble, she can introduce the ball and practice the step with one dribble. The player must remember to dribble the ball below the waist and in front of the jab step.

- After the player demonstrates that she can simultaneously coordinate the **crossover step** with the **dribble,** the player simulates steps 3, 4, and 5 by walking and counting each step out loud. The player finishes the walking drive by simulating a shot.

- Once the player has demonstrated that she has coordinated all five steps to the basket with only one dribble and is shooting off the correct foot, she can practice the entire five-step drive at game speed.

CHAPTER 12

Practice Drill

Scan this QR code for a video of the "Driving Layups" Practice Drill.

Driving Layups

Determining the Player's Minimum Goal

- A set is defined as ten attempted driving layups.

- The drill begins with the player taking three sets of driving layups and then adding the number of layups made in each set and dividing by three.

- The average number of driving layups made becomes the player's baseline score and his minimum goal.

- Young players who may have an undeveloped left or right hand should continue to use their underdeveloped hand throughout the drill even though it may depress their baseline score.

- The player's minimum goal in all practice drills is to achieve the baseline score.

- A player improves his ability to shoot layups by drilling the fundamentals of that skill based on the minimum and maximum goals that have been established rather than by practicing those skills without any goals and only on random occasions.

- If after three to five sets the player has not achieved his minimum goal, he should pause, move on to another drill, and then return to the drill.

- If the player continues to fail to reach his minimum goal, he should reassess his baseline score and establish a new minimum goal by averaging the scores of his past three sets.

Determining the Player's Maximum Goal

- The player's maximum goal is to surpass his baseline score by at least two made shots.

- If the player's baseline score is making six driving layups out of ten attempts, the player's maximum goal should be making eight driving layups out of ten attempts.

- Once the player consistently exceeds his maximum goal, he should increase his maximum goal by two made shots.

Driving Layups Diagrams

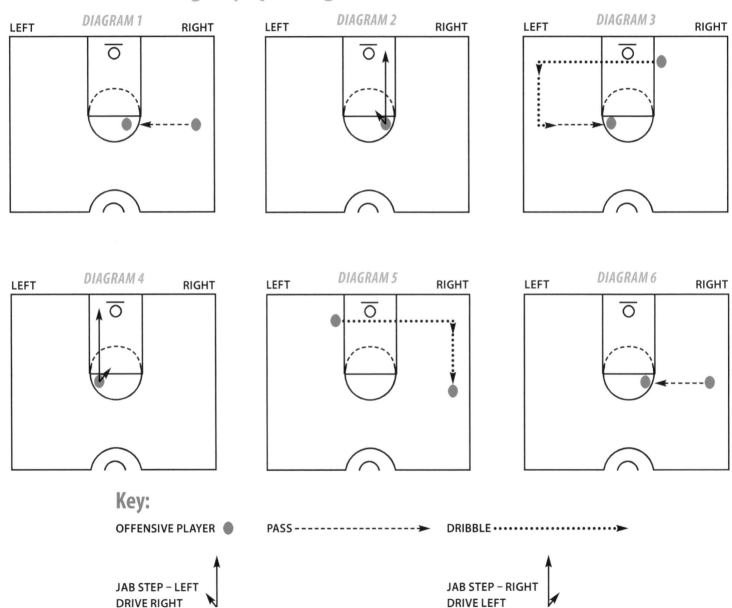

DIAGRAM 1   LEFT   RIGHT

DIAGRAM 2   LEFT   RIGHT

DIAGRAM 3   LEFT   RIGHT

DIAGRAM 4   LEFT   RIGHT

DIAGRAM 5   LEFT   RIGHT

DIAGRAM 6   LEFT   RIGHT

Key:

OFFENSIVE PLAYER   PASS   DRIBBLE

JAB STEP – LEFT
DRIVE RIGHT

JAB STEP – RIGHT
DRIVE LEFT

Diagram 1

The player starts at the right wing (foul line extended) five or six feet from where the foul lane meets the foul line.

The player throws a self-pass, hops to the ball, faces up, freezes the defender, and creates space.

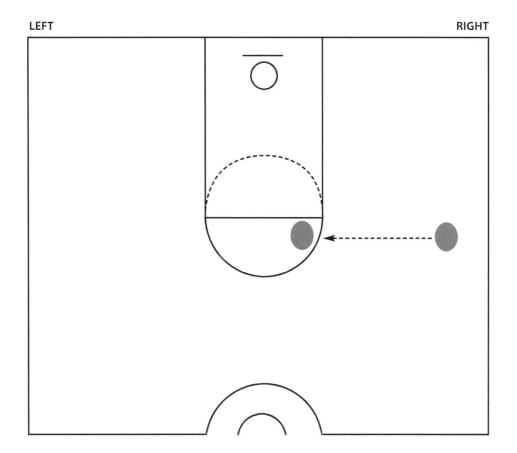

Diagram 2

On the **right** side of the court the player jab steps with his **left foot**.

Immediately after the jab step, the player steps with his l**eft foot** so that his left foot is pointing toward the basket and not toward the right side of the court.

As the player steps with his left foot, he simultaneously takes his dribble.

The player drives to the basket taking only one dribble and shoots the ball with his **right hand** and **right foot** raised in the air.

LEFT   RIGHT

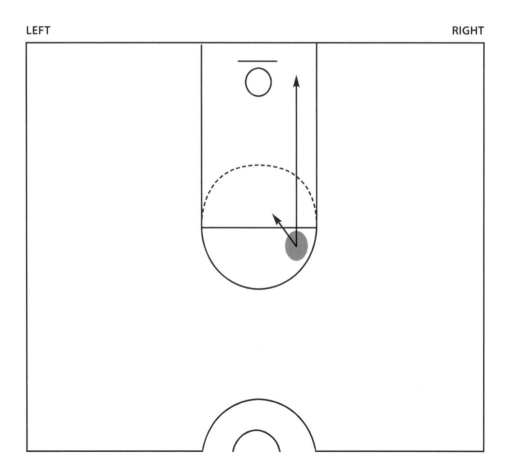

Diagram 3

The player rebounds his shot and immediately dribbles with his **right hand** along the baseline toward the left sideline and up the sideline until he reaches the wing on the left side of the court.

The player dribbles with his right hand with the same intensity as if he is being guarded.

When he reaches the wing on the left side of the court, the player will once again throw a self-pass, hop to the ball, face up, freeze the defender, and create space.

LEFT   **RIGHT**

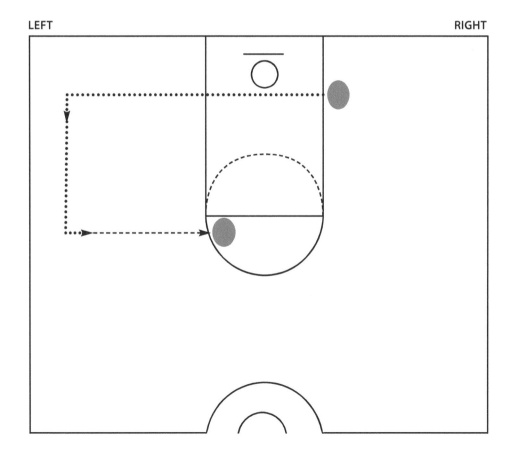

Diagram 4

On the **left** side of the court the player jab steps with his **right foot**.

Immediately after the jab step, the player steps with his **right foot** so that his right foot is pointing toward the basket and not toward the left side of the court.

As the player steps with his right foot, he simultaneously takes his dribble.

The player drives to the basket taking only one dribble and shoots the ball with his **left hand** and **left foot** raised in the air.

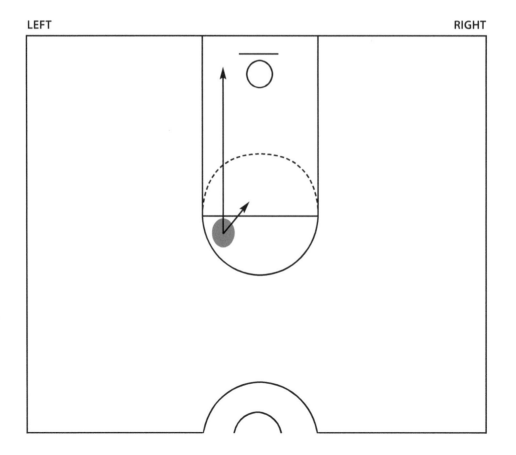

Diagram 5

The player rebounds his shot and immediately dribbles with his **left hand** along the baseline toward the right sideline and up the right sideline until he reaches the wing on the right side of the court.

The player dribbles with his left hand with the same intensity as if he is being guarded.

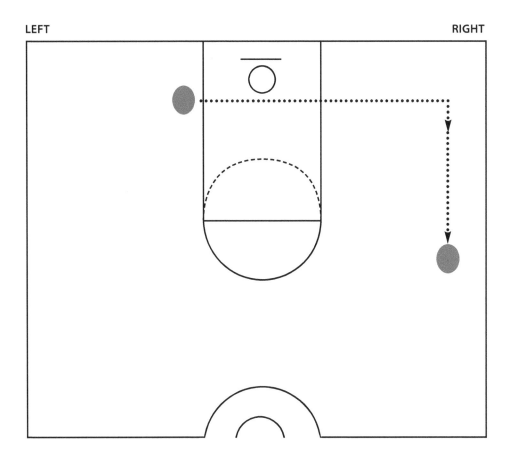

Diagram 6

When he reaches the wing on the right side of the court, the player will once again throw a self-pass, hop to the ball, face up, freeze the defender, and create space.

The player shoots a total of ten layups: five on the right side of the court and five on the left side of the court.

The player should keep a mental record of how many driving layups he makes.

The minimum goal is to reach his baseline score, and his maximum goal is to exceed his baseline score by two made shots. If the player consistently makes ten out of ten shots, he can increase his shot attempts to twelve.

After taking the driving layups, the player shoots two foul shots.

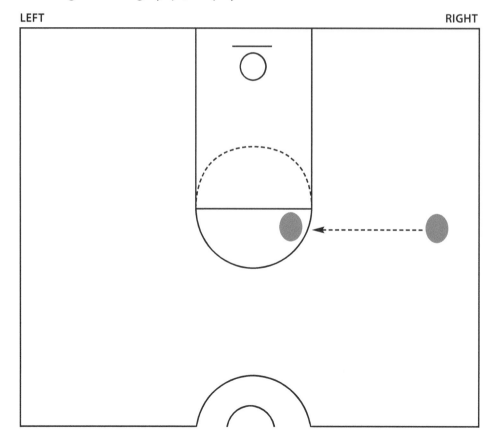

LEFT   RIGHT

CHAPTER 13

Shooting
Right Hand

A successful shot requires being square to the basket and proper use of the hands, arms, and legs. The legs provide strength and body balance, and the hands and arms provide the shot with an arc and follow-through.

THE FEET

The shooter's entire body—but specifically his two feet—must not only be balanced but must also be facing the basket. To use the vernacular, the shooter must be "square to the basket."

Shooting – Right Hand

THE KNEES

Young players must get the extra strength needed to reach a ten-foot-high basket by bending their knees and using the lower part of their body for leverage.

Knees

Shooting – Right Hand

THE SHOOTING HAND

The shooting hand must be centered on top of the ball, and the ball must be cradled in the fingertips and only slightly touching the palm of the shooting hand.

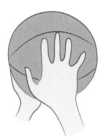

THE GUIDE HAND

The guide hand must be centered on the side of the ball with the seams of the basketball running horizontally.

Shooting – Right Hand
THE RELEASE POINT

To ensure that the player's shot has an arc and follow-through, the release point—the point where the ball leaves the shooter's hand—should be approximately between the shooter's nose and a hand's length above the shooter's head.

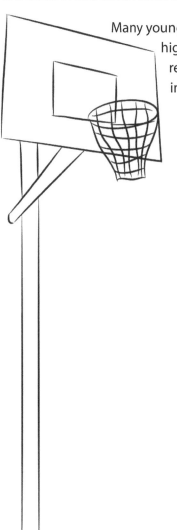

Many young players who lack the strength to reach a ten-foot-high basket will attempt to gain that strength by releasing the ball from their waist, which will result in a baseball-like throw or a high moon shot.

Shooting – Right Hand

THE FOLLOW-THROUGH

The final part of the shot is the follow-through, which requires a full extension of the shooter's hand and fingers.

Shooting
Left Hand

A successful shot requires being square to the basket and proper use of the hands, arms, and legs. The legs provide strength and body balance, and the hands and arms provide the shot with an arc and follow-through.

THE FEET

The shooter's entire body—but specifically her two feet—must not only be balanced but must also be facing the basket. To use the vernacular, the shooter must be "square to the basket."

THE KNEES

Young players must get the extra strength needed to reach a ten-foot-high basket by bending their knees and using the lower part of their body for leverage.

Knees

Shooting – Left Hand

The shooting hand must be centered on top of the ball, and the ball must be cradled in the fingertips and only slightly touching the palm of the shooting hand.

The guide hand must be centered on the side of the ball with the seams of the basketball running horizontally.

Shooting – Left Hand

THE RELEASE POINT

To ensure that the player's shot has an arc and follow-through, the release point—the point where the ball leaves the shooter's hand—should be approximately between the shooter's nose and a hand's length above the shooter's head.

Many young players who lack the strength to reach a ten-foot-high basket will attempt to gain that strength by releasing the ball from their waist, which will result in a baseball-like throw or a high moon shot.

Shooting – Left Hand

THE FOLLOW-THROUGH

The final part of the shot is the follow-through, which requires a full extension of the shooter's hand and fingers.

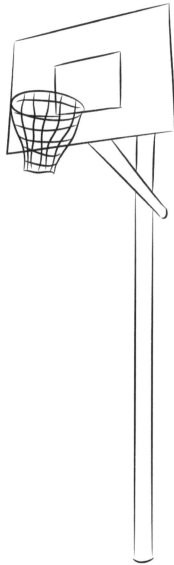

CHAPTER 14

Practice Drill
Six-Step Shooting

Scan this QR code for a video of the "Six-Step Shooting" Practice Drill.

The following **six-step drill** can teach young players how to coordinate the movements of their feet, knees, and hands.

Step 1

- The player stands next to a wall with a ball wedged between the spine of his back and the wall.

- The player visualizes himself balanced and square to the basket.

- The player holds a second ball at his waist with his shooting hand centered on top of the ball and his guide hand centered on the side of the ball.

Step 2

The player slowly bends and lowers his body, keeping the ball wedged between the wall and his back.

Step 3

The player begins to slowly rise up, keeping the ball wedged between the wall and his back while moving the ball to his chin.

Step 4

The player continues to rise up while simultaneously raising the ball to his forehead.

Step 5

The player rises to his full height, and using only the fingers of his shooting hand, flips the ball slightly above his forehead.

Step 6

The player releases the ball with a full follow-through and catches the ball before it hits the floor.

The player repeats these actions multiple times in succession.

Full sequence of the six-step drill

CHAPTER 15
Practice Drill
Layups Under the Basket

Scan this QR code for a video of the "Layups Under the Basket" Practice Drill.

Determining the Player's Minimum Goal

- A set is defined as the number of layups a player can make consecutively without missing.

- The drill begins with the player taking three sets of layups under the basket and then adding the number of layups made in each set and dividing by three.

- The average number of layups made becomes the player's baseline score and his minimum goal.

- Young players who may have an undeveloped left or right hand should continue the drill until the player misses with his dominant hand.

- The player's minimum goal in all practice drills is to achieve his baseline score.

- A player improves his ability to shoot layups by drilling the fundamentals of that skill based on the minimum and maximum goals that have been established rather than by practicing those skills without any goals and only on random occasions.

- If after three to five sets the player has not achieved his minimum goal, he should pause, move on to another drill, and then return to the drill.

- If on subsequent occasions the player continues to fail to reach his minimum goal, he should reassess his baseline score and establish a new minimum goal by averaging the scores of his past three sets.

Determining the Player's Maximum Goal

- The player's maximum goal is to surpass his baseline score by at least two made shots.

- If the player's baseline score is making ten consecutive layups, the player's maximum goal should be making twelve consecutive layups.

- Once the player consistently exceeds his maximum goal, he should increase his maximum goal by two made shots.

Points of Emphasis

RIGHT HAND, RIGHT FOOT; LEFT HAND, LEFT FOOT

- When shooting with the **right** hand, the player's **right** foot must be off the ground and the player pushes off of his **left** foot.

- When shooting with the **left** hand, the player's **left** foot must be off the ground and the player pushes off of his **right** foot.

- The player should not drop his arms after shooting the layup but should keep his arms raised as he moves from side to side.

- The player should not bring the ball down while rebounding and moving side to side.

- The player should keep his body square to the basket as he shoots the layups.

- When shooting, the player should keep the ball in front of his face and not shoot the ball from behind his ear.

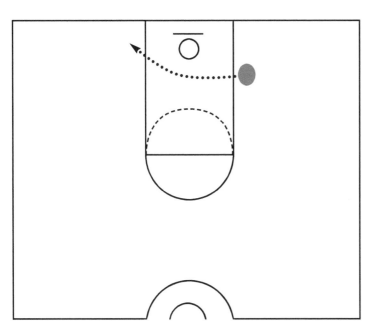 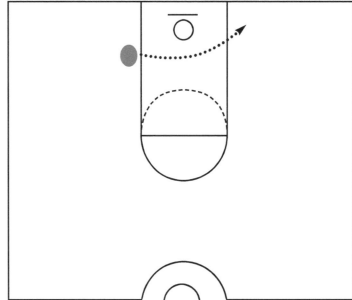

Instructions

- The player starts on the box on the right foul lane.

- The player shoots a layup with the right hand.

- The player rebounds the made shot.

- The player takes a step to the left side of the basket and shoots a layup with the left hand.

- The player continues to move side to side shooting layups while simultaneously counting how many layups he has made consecutively.

- If a layup is missed, the player stops, takes two foul shots, and starts shooting layups again.

- The player continues the drill until he has achieved his minimum or maximum goals. If after three to five minutes the player has not reached his minimum baseline score, the player stops and moves to the next drill.

- The player always finishes each drill with two foul shots.

CHAPTER 16

Foul Shot

Right Hand

The Fundamentals of Foul Shooting

- Hands are on the ball.

- Feet are square to the basket.

- Knees are bent.

- Player raises arms to the release point.

- Player follows through and shoots.

Shooting hand on top of the ball

Guide hand on the side of the ball

Body square to the basket

Foul Shot – Right Hand

THE KNEES

As the player bends his knees, he simultaneously lowers his arms but not below his waist.

Foul Shot – Right Hand

As the player straightens up, he simultaneously raises his arms and releases the ball from his forehead.

Foul Shot – Right Hand

THE FOLLOW-THROUGH

The player shoots the ball off his fingertips and follows through by bending his fingers down so they are pointing forward.

Foul Shot
Left Hand
The Fundamentals of Foul Shooting

- Hands are on the ball.

- Feet are square to the basket.

- Knees are bent.

- Player raises arms to the release point.

- Player follows through and shoots.

Guide hand on the side of the ball

Shooting hand on top of the ball

Body square to the basket

Foul Shot – Left Hand

THE KNEES

As the player bends her knees, she simultaneously lowers her arms but not below her waist.

Foul Shot – Left Hand

THE RELEASE POINT

As the player straightens up, she simultaneously raises her arms and releases the ball from her forehead.

Foul Shot – Left Hand

THE FOLLOW-THROUGH

The player shoots the ball off her fingertips and follows through by bending her fingers down so they are pointing forward.

CHAPTER 17

Stand-Still Jump Shot
Right Hand
BODY BALANCE

- Feet and body must be square to the basket.

- Right foot and left foot must be parallel.

- The seams of the basketball should be running horizontally.

Stand-Still Jump Shot – Right Hand

THE RELEASE POINT

● The player raises his arms above the forehead while simultaneously rising off the floor.

Stand-Still Jump Shot – Right Hand

THE FOLLOW-THROUGH

- Do not drop the guide hand.

- Maintain the follow-through by lowering the fingers of the shooting hand so they are not facing up but facing forward.

Stand-Still Jump Shot – Right Hand

THE LANDING

When the shooter lands:

● His feet should be parallel.

● His body should be square to the basket.

Stand-Still Jump Shot
Left Hand
BODY BALANCE

- Feet and body must be square to the basket.

- Right foot and left foot must be parallel.

- The seams of the basketball should be running horizontally.

Stand-Still Jump Shot – Left Hand

THE RELEASE POINT

- The player raises her arms above the forehead while simultaneously rising off the floor.

Stand-Still Jump Shot – Left Hand

THE FOLLOW-THROUGH

- Do not drop the guide hand.

- Maintain the follow-through by lowering the fingers of the shooting hand so they are not facing up but facing forward.

Stand-Still Jump Shot – Left Hand

THE LANDING

When the shooter lands:

- Her feet should be parallel.

- Her body should be square to the basket.

CHAPTER 18
Practice Drill
Stand-Still Jump Shots

Scan this QR code for a video of the "Stand-Still Jump Shots" Practice Drill.

Determining the Player's Minimum Goal

- A set is defined as ten attempted jump shots.

- The drill begins with the player taking three sets of jump shots and then adding the number of jump shots made in each set and dividing by three.

- The average number of jump shots made becomes the player's baseline score and his minimum goal.

- The player's minimum goal in all practice drills is to achieve the baseline score.

- A player improves his ability to shoot jump shots by drilling the fundamentals of that skill based on the minimum and maximum goals that have been established rather than by practicing those skills without any goals and only on random occasions.

- If after three to five sets the player has not achieved his minimum goal, he should pause, move on to another drill, and then return to the drill.

- If on subsequent occasions the player continues to fail to reach his minimum goal, he should reassess his baseline score and establish a new minimum goal by averaging the scores of his past three sets.

Determining the Player's Maximum Goal

- The player's maximum goal is to surpass his baseline score by at least two made shots.

- If the player's baseline score is making six jump shots out of ten attempts, the player's maximum goal should be making eight jump shots out of ten attempts.

- Once the player consistently exceeds his maximum goal, he should increase his maximum goal by two made shots.

Stand-Still Jump Shots Diagrams

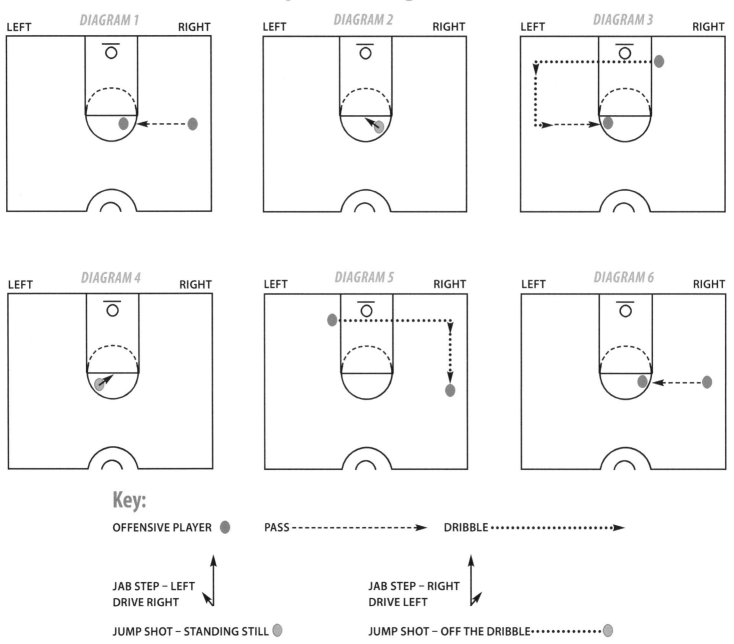

Key:

OFFENSIVE PLAYER ●   PASS ------------>   DRIBBLE ••••••••••>

JAB STEP – LEFT
DRIVE RIGHT

JAB STEP – RIGHT
DRIVE LEFT

JUMP SHOT – STANDING STILL ●

JUMP SHOT – OFF THE DRIBBLE ••••••••••••●

Diagram 1

The player starts at the right wing (foul line extended) five or six feet from where the foul lane meets the foul line.

The player throws a self-pass, hops to the ball, faces up, freezes the defender, and creates space.

LEFT   RIGHT

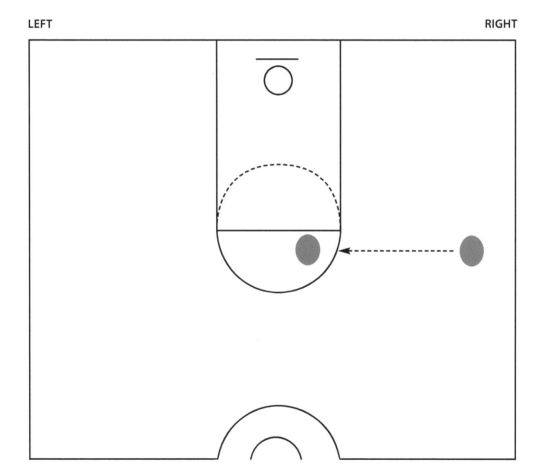

Diagram 2

On the **right** side of the court the player jab steps with his **left foot**.

Immediately after the jab step, the player faces up and shoots a jump shot.

The player rebounds his shot.

LEFT   **RIGHT**

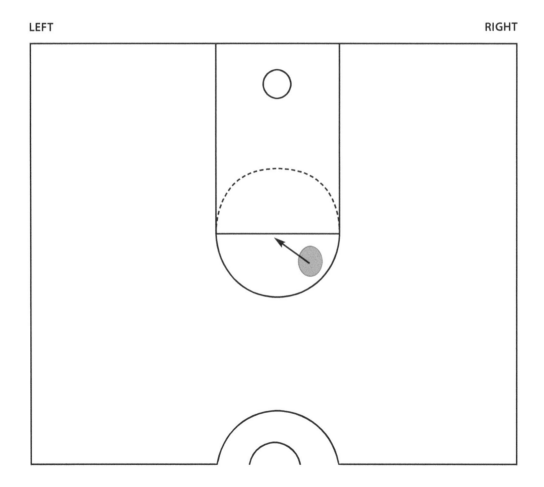

Diagram 3

The player dribbles with his right hand along the baseline toward the left sideline and up the sideline until he reaches the wing on the left side of the court.

The player dribbles with his right hand with the same intensity as if he is being guarded.

When he reaches the wing on the left side of the court, the player will once again throw a self-pass, hop to the ball, face up, freeze the defender, and create space.

LEFT **RIGHT**

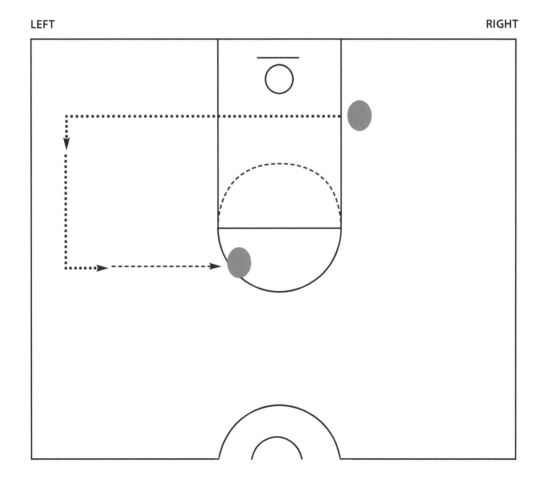

Diagram 4

On the **left** side of the court the player jab steps with his **right foot**.

Immediately after the jab step, the player faces up and shoots a jump shot.

The player rebounds his shot.

LEFT   **RIGHT**

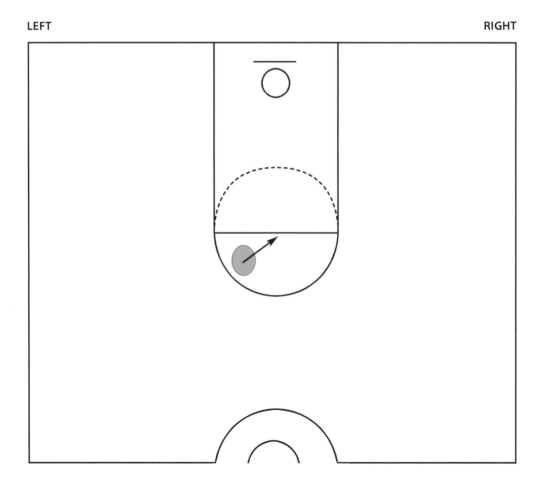

Diagram 5

The player dribbles with his left hand along the baseline toward the right sideline and up the right sideline until he reaches the wing on the right side of the court.

The player dribbles with his left hand with the same intensity as if he is being guarded.

LEFT   **RIGHT**

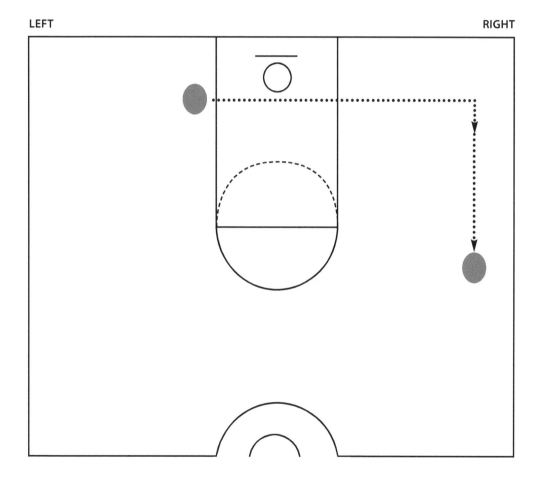

Diagram 6

When he reaches the wing on the right side of the court, the player will once again throw a self-pass, hop to the ball, face up, freeze the defender, and create space.

The player shoots a total of ten jump shots: five on the right side of the court and five on the left side of the court.

The player should keep a mental record of how many jump shots he makes.

The minimum goal is to reach his baseline score, and his maximum goal is to exceed his baseline score by two made jump shots. If the player consistently makes ten out of ten jump shots, the player can increase the shot attempts to twelve.

After taking ten jump shots, the player shoots two foul shots.

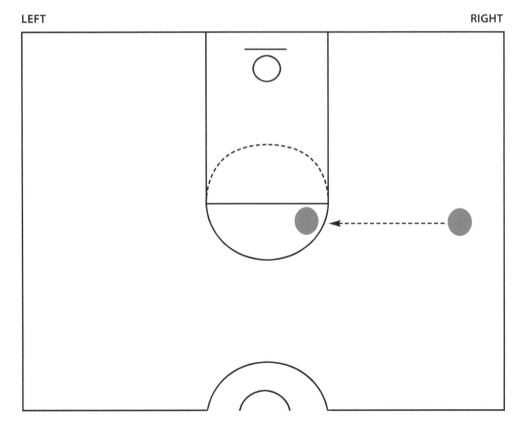

LEFT   RIGHT

CHAPTER 19
Why You Miss — How To Self-Correct

If a player wants to know why he missed a shot, he must first determine whether the shot missed to the **LEFT**, to the **RIGHT**, was **LONG,** or was **SHORT**.

Right Hand

If the missed shot hits the **LEFT** side of the rim, the player's shooting hand may be on the side of the ball and not on top of the ball.

INCORRECT

CORRECT
The shooting hand is on top of ball.

Why You Miss – How To Self-Correct – Right Hand

If the missed shot hits the **RIGHT** side of the rim, the player's feet may not be square to the basket but pointing to the left.

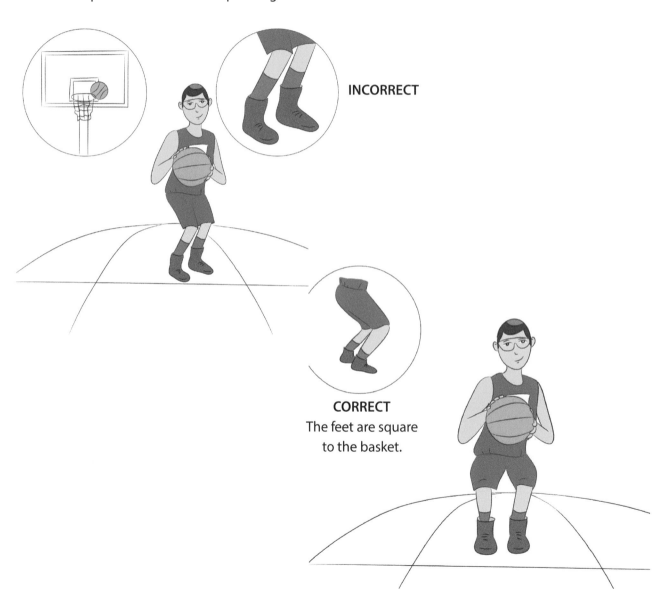

INCORRECT

CORRECT
The feet are square
to the basket.

Why You Miss – How To Self-Correct – Right Hand

If the missed shot hits the **RIGHT** side of the rim, the player's hand may not be square to the rim but turned to the side and pointing straight up.

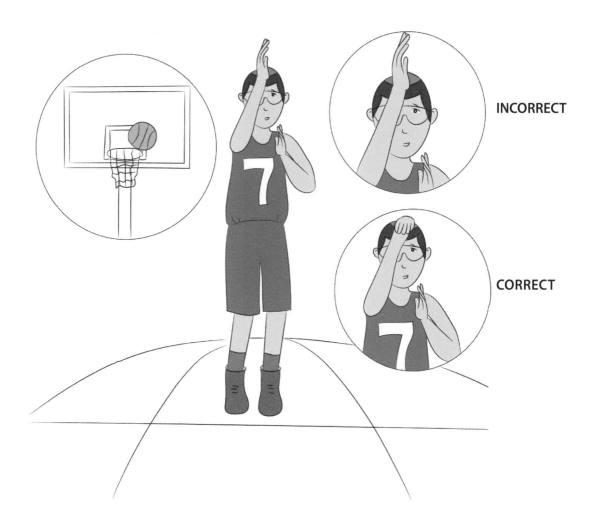

INCORRECT

CORRECT

Why You Miss – How To Self-Correct – Right Hand

If the missed shot is **LONG** and hits the backboard, the player's shooting and guide hands may be on the sides of the ball or under the ball.

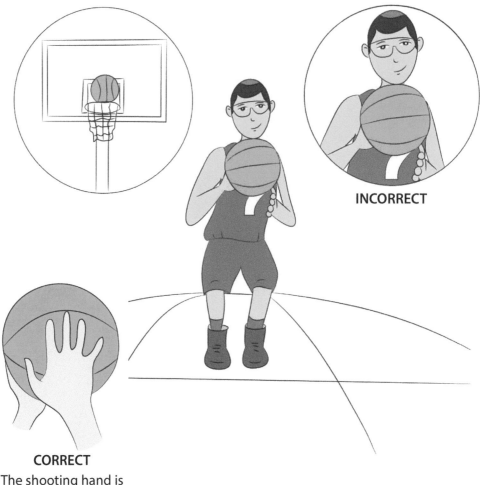

INCORRECT

CORRECT
The shooting hand is
on top of ball.

Why You Miss – How To Self-Correct – Right Hand

If the missed shot is **LONG** and hits the back of the rim or the backboard, the player's release point may be too high and above the head.

INCORRECT

CORRECT
The release point is at the forehead.

Why You Miss – How To Self-Correct – Right Hand

If the missed shot is too **LONG** and hits the back of the rim or the backboard, the player's follow-through may not have a full extension and the ball will have no reverse spin.

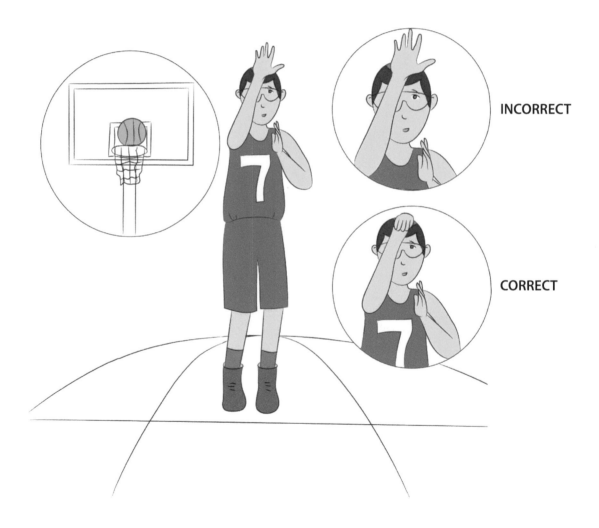

INCORRECT

CORRECT

Why You Miss – How To Self-Correct – Right Hand

If the missed shot is **SHORT** and hits the front of the rim, the player's release point may be below the chin and the player's knees may not be bent enough.

INCORRECT

CORRECT
The release point is at the forehead and the knees are bent.

Why You Miss – How To Self-Correct

If a player wants to know why she missed a shot, she must first determine whether the shot missed to the **RIGHT**, to the **LEFT**, was **LONG**, or was **SHORT**.

Left Hand

If the missed shot hits the **RIGHT** side of the rim, the player's shooting hand may be on the side of the ball and not on top of the ball.

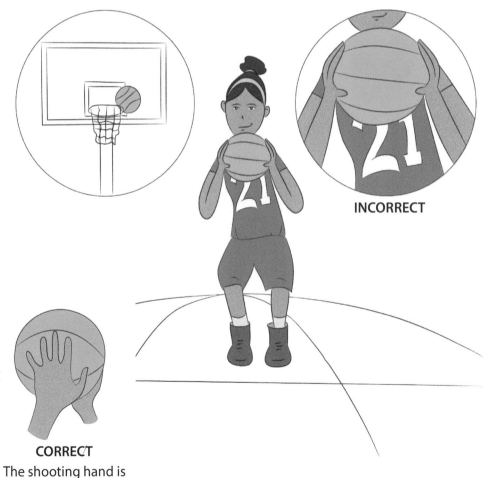

INCORRECT

CORRECT
The shooting hand is
on top of ball.

Why You Miss – How To Self-Correct – Left Hand

If the missed shot hits the **LEFT** side of the rim, the player's feet may not be square to the basket but pointing to the right.

INCORRECT

CORRECT
The feet are square
to the basket.

Why You Miss – How To Self-Correct – Left Hand

If the missed shot hits the **LEFT** side of the rim, the player's hand may not be square to the rim but turned to the side and pointing straight up.

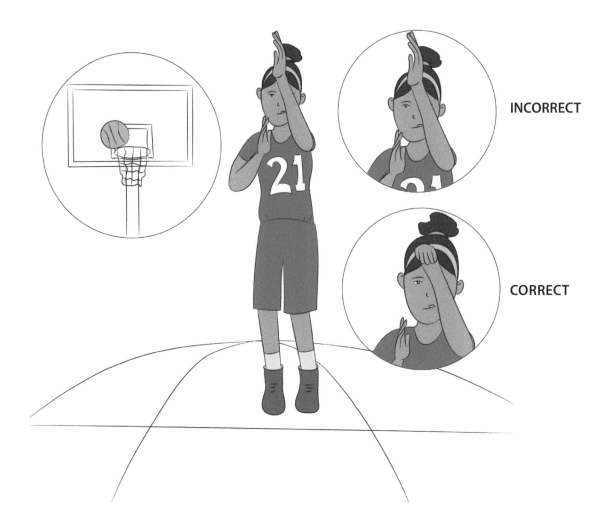

INCORRECT

CORRECT

Why You Miss – How To Self-Correct – Left Hand

If the missed shot is **LONG** and hits the backboard, the player's shooting and guide hands may be on the sides of the ball or under the ball.

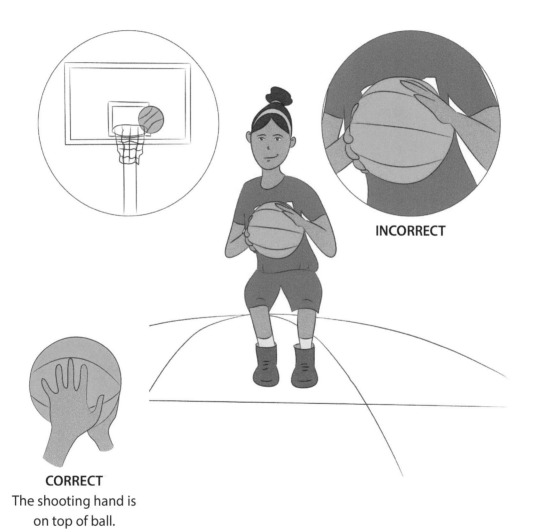

INCORRECT

CORRECT
The shooting hand is
on top of ball.

Why You Miss – How To Self-Correct – Left Hand

If the missed shot is **LONG** and hits the back of the rim or the backboard, the player's release point may be too high and above the head.

INCORRECT

CORRECT
The release point is at the forehead.

Why You Miss – How To Self-Correct – Left Hand

If the missed shot is too **LONG** and hits the back of the rim or the backboard, the player's follow-through may not have a full extension and the ball will have no reverse spin.

INCORRECT

CORRECT

Why You Miss – How To Self-Correct – Left Hand

If the missed shot is **SHORT** and hits the front of the rim, the player's release point may be below the chin and the player's knees may not be bent enough.

INCORRECT

CORRECT
The release point is at the forehead and the knees are bent.

About the Author

Jonathan Halpert played college basketball for Yeshiva University's legendary coach Red Sarachek from 1962 to 1966 and began his college coaching career in 1972. He was winner of the College Basketball Officials Association Sportsmanship Award in 1980 and 1997, was named Skyline Conference Coach of the Year in 2000 and 2010, was the recipient of the Metropolitan Basketball Writers "Good Guy" Award in 1998 and the Metropolitan Basketball Writers Association Distinguished Service Award in 2015.

Upon his retirement in 2013 he was the longest-tenured college coach in New York City history and fourth among all currently active NCAA coaches. In 2012, he became the seventh coach in New York City history to earn 400 victories.

He received a BA and BHL degree from Yeshiva College in 1966, an MA degree in Educational Psychology from New York University in 1967, and a PhD in Special Education from Yeshiva University's Ferkauf Graduate School of Humanities and Social Sciences in 1978.

He is the author of *Are You Still Coaching? 41 Years Coaching Yeshiva University Basketball; Backdoor Hoops: The Lost Art of Moving Without the Ball;* and *So You Want To Be a Coach: A Collection of Essays on the Challenges That Await New and Experienced Coaches.*

He is married to the former Aviva Margolis, has five children, twenty grandchildren, and three great-grandchildren.

Coach Halpert is available for coaching workshops, team clinics, and individualized instruction. For further information, e-mail: mamboa30@hotmail.com

Scan this QR code for a video of Johnny Halpert's concluding statement to all grandparents.

About the Illustrator

Sari Kopitnikoff is a digital artist, experiential educator, and content creator. She's the creator of *That Jewish Moment*, a collection of original illustrations, programs, and materials celebrating Jewish life. You can find her on social media @thatjewishmoment.

Production Team

INTERIOR AND COVER DESIGN

Andrea Leigh Ptak, www.andrealeighptak.com, andrealeighptak@me.com

COPY EDITOR/PROOFREADER

Nancy Silk, nancy.silk842@gmail.com

VIDEOS PRODUCED BY

RUX MEDIA, www.ruxmedia.com

COMPUTER OPERATIONS

Jason Goldfarb, www.clockbuildermedia.com

VIDEO DEMONSTRATIONS PERFORMED BY

Aryeh Halpert, Yeshiva University Varsity Basketball Team 2021–2022

ASSISTANT DEMONSTRATORS

Talia Baratz, Naomi Butler, Dani Goldfarb, Elie Goldfarb, Alyssa Halpert, Ari Halpert, Ben Halpert, Ezra Halpert, Josh Halpert

FUTURE DEMONSTRATORS

Ava Baratz, Dovi Hirt, Orly Hirt

FOCUS GROUPS

Aviva Halpert, *Chairperson*
Tzippora and David Baratz; Ariella and Jonah Kaszovitz;
Tzofit and Jason Goldfarb; Shoshana and Yehuda Halpert;
Michelle and Rafi Halpert; Shimona Shriki;
Talia and Eytan Baratz; Yael Baratz; Aliza and Evan Goldstein; Avigayil Halpert;
Leora Halpert; Daniella and Elie Hirt; Shelley and Nachshon Kaszovitz;
Yair Kaszovitz; Yedida Kaszovitz; Avital and Tal Sharon

Are You Still Coaching?

The nine members of the 1975–1976 Yeshiva University varsity basketball team attended their Jewish studies classes from 9:00 to 1:00, their secular classes from 2:00 to 7:00, practiced until 10:00, and went on to become doctors, dentists, or lawyers. The 1975 team's daily schedule and accomplishments were not unique, but rather representative of the approximately six hundred players who for eighty-three years have worn the Yeshiva University blue and white uniform . . .

The stories in chapter 11, "Why They Played," describe what happens when Yeshiva players attempt to find time for everything: Torah study, secular knowledge, and athletic triumph.

Are You Still Coaching?

41 Years Coaching
Yeshiva University Basketball

Johnny Halpert

Praise for *Are You Still Coaching?...*

"When Dr. Halpert scours the globe for good player–athletes who will lead the team to victory, he looks for athletic promise, but in searching for the best, he is cognizant that, in the final analysis, his team will be the YU team. He knows that the players must be the best, but also informed by values—Jewish values, universal values, and values touched by the breath of Torah."

Rabbi Simcha Krauss, Rabbi Emeritus, Young Israel of Hillcrest

"The passion is there because the game of basketball is that kind of game. Coach Halpert exemplifies that spirit because he can get excited—and if you don't get excited, then the players won't get excited. He is able to translate that feeling and inner love to the players."

Lou Carnesecca, St. John's University

Coming Soon...
Backdoor Hoops

The Lost Art of Moving Without the Ball

By Johnny Halpert

Successful players and great teams instinctively use the fundamentals of moving without the ball, and now, finally, there is a book that explains and illustrates these fundamentals. *Back Door Hoops* should be required reading for all players and coaches looking to up their game. Nice Job, Coach.

Earl "the Pearl" Monroe, *NY Knickerbockers 1971–1980, NBA Hall of Fame 1990*

So You Want to Be a Coach

A Collection of Essays on the Challenges That Await New and Experienced Coaches

By Johnny Halpert

Lightning Source UK Ltd.
Milton Keynes UK
UKHW050251041022
409848UK00002B/64